THE LONG WHITE CLOUD

Stories from New Zealand

The stories in this book look at life at both ends. First there is Walter, six years old, always asking questions, wanting to find out things that adults don't want him to know. At the other end of life are Mr and Mrs Blackie, looking for ways to show each other what is in their hearts. Then there is Roy, alone and lonely, roaring into the night on his motorbike. And the fourth story is a Māori family, grandson and grandfather, gathering the *whakapapa*, the long history of their family. For the Māori people go back many centuries, into the misty past, to the time when the first canoes came over the sea to *Aotearoa*, the land of the long white cloud.

BOOKWORMS WORLD STORIES

English has become an international language, and is used on every continent, in many varieties, for all kinds of purposes. *Bookworms World Stories* are the latest addition to the Oxford Bookworms Library. Their aim is to bring the best of the world's stories to the English language learner, and to celebrate the use of English for storytelling all around the world.

Jennifer Bassett
Series Editor

Christine Lindop would like to thank the following for their assistance with the research for this volume: Virginia Gallagher in New Zealand; Vicky Eccott and staff at the British Empire and Commonwealth Museum, Bristol, UK

OXFORD BOOKWORMS LIBRARY
World Stories

The Long White Cloud

Stories from New Zealand

Stage 3 (1000 headwords)

Series Editor: Jennifer Bassett
Founder Editor: Tricia Hedge
Activities Editors: Jennifer Bassett and Christine Lindop

For Jinny
keeper of the whakapapa

RETOLD BY CHRISTINE LINDOP

The Long White Cloud
Stories from New Zealand

Illustrated by
Chris King

OXFORD UNIVERSITY PRESS

OXFORD
UNIVERSITY PRESS

Great Clarendon Street, Oxford OX2 6DP

Oxford University Press is a department of the University of Oxford.
It furthers the University's objective of excellence in research, scholarship,
and education by publishing worldwide in

Oxford New York

Auckland Cape Town Dar es Salaam Hong Kong Karachi
Kuala Lumpur Madrid Melbourne Mexico City Nairobi
New Delhi Shanghai Taipei Toronto

With offices in

Argentina Austria Brazil Chile Czech Republic France Greece
Guatemala Hungary Italy Japan Poland Portugal Singapore
South Korea Switzerland Thailand Turkey Ukraine Vietnam

OXFORD and OXFORD ENGLISH are registered trade marks of
Oxford University Press in the UK and in certain other countries

ISBN: 978 0 19 479139 7

A complete recording of this Bookworms edition of *The Long White Cloud:
Stories from New Zealand* is available on audio CD ISBN 978 0 19 479104 5

Printed in Hong Kong

ACKNOWLEDGEMENTS

The publishers are grateful to the following for permission to adapt and simplify copyright texts:
Antony Fanshawe for *After the Earthquake* by James Courage (first published in the journal
Landfall in 1948); Philip Mincher for *A Kind of Longing*; Joy Cowley for *The Silk*; Witi Ihimaera
(Richards Literary Agency) for *Gathering of the Whakapapa*, which was first published by Reed
Publishing NZ in *The New Net Goes Fishing* (1977) and is currently in *Kingfisher Come Home* (1995)

Word count (main text): 11,150 words

For more information on the Oxford Bookworms Library,
visit www.oup.com/elt/bookworms

CONTENTS

A71681

INTRODUCTION   i

NOTE ON THE LANGUAGE   viii

After the Earthquake   1

James Courage

Gathering of the Whakapapa   17

Witi Ihimaera

A Kind of Longing   27

Philip Mincher

The Silk   43

Joy Cowley

GLOSSARY   57

ACTIVITIES: Before Reading   60

ACTIVITIES: After Reading   62

ABOUT THE AUTHORS   67

ABOUT THE BOOKWORMS LIBRARY   69

NOTE ON THE LANGUAGE

There are many varieties of English spoken in the world, and the characters in these stories from New Zealand sometimes use non-standard forms (for example, leaving out auxiliary verbs such as *are* and *is*). This is how the authors of the original stories represented the spoken language that their characters would actually use in real life.

There are also words that are usually only found in New Zealand English (for example, *fullas*), and in the story by Witi Ihimaera, a Māori writer, there are a few words from the Māori language. All these words are either explained in the stories or in the glossary on pages 57 to 59.

After the Earthquake

JAMES COURAGE

∎

Retold by Christine Lindop

More than a century ago, many people from Britain sailed out to New Zealand, to start new lives as farmers or doctors or teachers. It was not a crowded country, and people on farms and in small towns all knew each other. They knew each other's family history, how much money they had, who loved whom, who hated whom . . .

Children, of course, must not know too much about what adults do and think and feel. But Walter, who is only six, notices things and likes to ask questions . . .

The earthquake happened late on a Saturday night in summer and shook the coast, the farms, and the towns for twenty miles, from the sea to the mountains. At the Blakiston home everybody had gone to bed and was asleep, but the shake woke Mr Blakiston immediately. When it was over, he sat up in bed, lit his candle, and looked about him at the walls and ceiling. He could not see any damage, although the quake had been strong and had shaken the house from side to side for a moment or two.

'Are you all right?' Mr Blakiston asked his wife, who was now awake beside him.

'Yes, dear, but do go and see if Walter is awake. He may be frightened.' She had been frightened herself, waking from a dream of ships on the sea.

Her husband rested on one elbow, staring at the candle and listening for sounds from his son's room. Walter was six and had his own room near the top of the stairs.

'He must be all right,' said Mr Blakiston, hearing no sound in the house. He blew out the candle and lay back beside his wife. 'Still, that was a bad little quake. Yes, a damn bad little quake.' Soon he was asleep again.

In the morning they found little damage outside, except for the old wash-house chimney, out at the back, which had fallen onto the wash-house roof. But inside the house a thin china vase had fallen onto the floor and broken. At breakfast time Mr Blakiston brought the pieces of the vase to the table, to show his wife and son.

'English china,' he explained to the boy. 'Very fine too. See that letter D? That's for Doulton, the people who made it.'

But Walter was more interested in the earthquake. 'Did the whole house shake?' he asked his father.

'Shook, yes, and went up and down a bit.'

'Do you think it shook down any houses that we know?'

'Not many – maybe a few ceilings and chimneys.'

Walter ate his breakfast. 'I'd like to see an earthquake,' he said. 'I'd like to see houses falling down, and all the people inside them getting frightened.'

'Walter,' said his mother, 'you shouldn't say things like that. It's very unkind. You should think first.'

'I did think first,' said Walter softly, to his plate.

'What did you say?' asked his mother. 'Speak clearly.'

'I only said I'm sorry I didn't wake up in the earthquake.'

That day was a Sunday. Mr Blakiston was a farmer, and although there is work to do on a farm every day of the week, he usually spent Sundays in and around the farm buildings near the house, resting himself. Every fourth Sunday the family went to church in the town down in the valley. But today Mr Blakiston, with Walter's help, began to clear the bricks from the roof of the wash-house, where the chimney had fallen.

Walter always asked questions when he worked with his father. 'Do earthquakes happen in England?' he asked.

'Yes,' said Mr Blakiston, 'But not often.' He was enjoying the work, and found Walter's questions a little boring. The broken vase made him think about England, the Old Country, and he wanted to think in silence.

He had had his farm in New Zealand for nearly twenty years, but he still thought of England as home. Colonial life was freer, and he liked it better, but it was not as English now as it used to be. Life was changing in this young country, and he was changing with it.

Now, as he threw the bricks from the roof down to the ground, he knew that he would never go back to England. He was a colonial farmer for life. Time had decided this for him, and he felt pleased.

'Can I drive to town with Mum in the morning?' asked Walter.

'Yes, if you want to. Now climb down and put those bricks tidily by the wall.'

*Walter always asked questions when he worked
with his father.*

. . .

Next morning at eleven o'clock Mr Blakiston brought the horse and gig to the front door. Every fine weekday morning at eleven Mrs Blakiston drove to the town four miles away to get the post and the newspaper and to shop at the store. Summer or winter, she wore a flat grey hat and long gloves.

On this Monday morning Walter went with her. They drove past wide flat fields of hot yellow grass, burnt by the sun, until they came to the town. Mrs Blakiston stopped the gig by the verandah of Lakin's General Store.

'Can I go in?' asked Walter, getting ready to jump down.

'Mr Lakin will be out in a moment,' said his mother. She opened her purse and found her shopping list. 'We'll wait till he comes.'

Soon Mr Lakin came out from the shop door. He held his hand above his eyes to keep off the bright sun and looked up at the gig. 'Good to see you're all right after the quake, Mrs Blakiston,' he said, in his high thin voice.

'I'm very well, Mr Lakin, but it did frighten us a little, so late at night. Did you have any damage?'

'I slept through it, myself. But I found a few broken bottles on the floor yesterday morning.'

Mrs Blakiston gave Mr Lakin her shopping list.

'Have you heard about old Mrs Duncaster?' he asked.

'Heard about her?' Mrs Blakiston was not sure.

'The quake brought the ceiling down on her. She died of shock, they say, early yesterday.'

'Oh, but what a terrible thing, Mr Lakin—' said Mrs Blakiston. 'I had no idea—'

'Well, it was a sudden end,' Mr Lakin said. 'I thought I should tell you,' he added. 'I don't like my old customers dying.'

'Yes,' said Mrs Blakiston. 'Thank you, Mr Lakin. I hadn't heard about it, of course. I'll go and visit her daughter this morning.'

Mr Lakin went to fetch Mrs Blakiston's shopping.

'The Mrs Duncaster who is dead,' said Walter, 'is she the old lady I know?'

'Yes,' said his mother. 'I'd no idea,' she added quietly to herself. 'Of course it was Sunday yesterday, so we didn't hear.'

'Did the roof fall right on her face in bed?'

'I don't know, Walter. Don't ask silly questions. You heard what Mr Lakin said.'

'I think when there's an earthquake you should get right under the blankets. Then the ceiling won't hurt you.'

'She was very old. It's very sad that she's dead,' said Mrs Blakiston. She pulled Walter's sunhat down to his eyes, and made him sit up straight on the hot seat of the gig.

'Are we going to visit Miss Duncaster?' he asked.

'Yes, we must go and see her. She loved her mother very much.'

After Mr Lakin had put the shopping in the back of the gig, Mrs Blakiston drove up the street to the post office to get the post and the newspaper. She then drove to the north end of the town, where the Duncasters lived.

A row of trees hid the little low house from the road. Behind the trees, long wild grass, burnt almost red by the sun, grew up to the verandah.

'There's somebody here already,' said Walter. A dark brown horse stood by the verandah, tied to one of the posts. It was a farmer's horse, a working horse.

Mrs Blakiston looked at the horse for a moment, then, carefully holding her long skirt, she got down from the gig and knocked at the door. She knocked twice, in the hot summer silence, before the door was opened by a tall woman in a dark grey dress.

Walter watched his mother kiss Miss Duncaster. He had hoped to see Miss Duncaster crying for a mother killed in an earthquake. But he was sorry to see that Annie Duncaster's light blue eyes and pink face looked just the same as usual.

'You must come in and have tea,' said Miss Duncaster's deep voice to his mother. 'And Walter with you. Please, please do. I'd like it.'

'But you have a visitor already,' said Mrs Blakiston.

Miss Duncaster looked quickly at the horse tied to the verandah. 'Nobody's here,' she said. 'Nobody at all. Please come in.'

So Mrs Blakiston put the gig under the trees, tied up the horse, and took Walter with her into the house. 'You must be quiet,' she whispered to Walter, 'and not ask questions.'

■ ■ ■

Inside the house it was dark and smelt cool after the hot morning. The little room behind the verandah was full of china and books, but the most interesting thing to Walter was a great creamy-white egg in a corner. It was bigger than his hands. When Miss Duncaster had brought in the tea, he sat down to stare at the wonderful egg while his mother talked.

'I've only just heard about your mother, Annie,' said Mrs Blakiston. 'I'm so very sorry.'

'Mother hated earthquakes,' Miss Duncaster said calmly. 'We had a bad one here, you know, just after father and she had first come from England. She had always been frightened of them since then.'

'They frighten me too. Did your mother die suddenly?'

'A little of the ceiling fell, you know, in her room. I got her out of bed and into a chair and ran downstairs to make her a cup of tea. When I got back, she was dead.' Miss Duncaster put down her cup and stared out of the window. 'It was all a great shock. The earthquake itself and then my mother dead.'

'I slept all through the earthquake,' said Walter, 'didn't I, Mum?'

'Yes, dear, luckily,' said his mother.

Miss Duncaster, who had begun to cry a little, suddenly seemed happier and said, 'Of course, my mother was no longer a young woman. But even at sixty, people like to live. And she had had a wonderful life. Young people like me can't hope for nearly so much.'

'Yes, Annie, I know,' said Mrs Blakiston, who also knew that old Mrs Duncaster had been at least seventy and that her daughter was at least thirty-five. 'It is hard for you, on your own now,' she added.

Miss Duncaster got up. 'Oh, thank you, thank you. But I won't let myself be lonely.' She looked quickly out of the window, then moved to the door. 'I'd like you to come and see my mother now,' she said. 'She's lying upstairs in father's old room. She looks beautiful.'

*Miss Duncaster put down her cup
and stared out of the window.*

'Yes, of course I'll come up,' said Mrs Blakiston. 'Walter, you stay down here for a few minutes.'

'Oh, but I want Walter to see her too,' said Miss Duncaster. 'She always loved children, you know.'

The stairs were very narrow and dark, and the air was warm up under the roof.

'In here,' said Miss Duncaster, opening a door.

The small bedroom was full of dark furniture and had a window in the roof. The bed was against the wall by the door, and on the bed, covered by a sheet up to her neck, lay the dead Mrs Duncaster. Walter was surprised; the round creamy-white face was like the big egg downstairs, he thought, but somebody had given it a nose and a mouth and put a hard line down each side. He hadn't remembered that old Mrs Duncaster looked so serious; she had always laughed at him and given him sweets.

On a table by the bed there was a vase full of green leaves and large open milky flowers that gave out a strong smell.

'Magnolias,' said Mrs Blakiston gently, her head on one side. She loved flowers. 'Beautiful,' she added.

'I picked them from the garden,' said Miss Duncaster. 'Mother planted the tree when I was born. It has grown up with me. I felt she'd like to have the flowers beside her now.'

'Yes,' said Mrs Blakiston, 'yes, Annie, of course.'

Walter turned away to look at a box made of dark shiny wood on the floor by the window.

'That belonged to my father,' explained Miss Duncaster. 'He was a doctor, you know – the first doctor in this town. All his doctor's things are in that box.'

'Did he come from England?' asked Walter.

'A long time ago, in a sailing ship, with my mother. Mother missed England all her life, but she didn't go back, even when father died.'

At that moment Walter noticed old Mrs Duncaster's hand on the side of the bed, lying just under the edge of the sheet. The hand held a book with something in gold on the cover. 'What's that?' he asked.

'My mother's Bible,' said Miss Duncaster.

'No, I meant the gold thing on the cover—'

'Oh, that's my mother's family crest. Yes, that meant a lot to her.' Miss Duncaster sighed, then added, to Walter's mother: 'She came from a very old, important English family, you know. I never knew any of them, of course. They meant nothing to me.' She pulled the sheet over the dead hand and straightened the magnolias in their vase. 'I'm a colonial,' she said. 'My life is here, in this country.'

Soon they went downstairs. 'Walter and I must go home now, Annie,' said Mrs Blakiston.

'You have been so kind,' said Miss Duncaster. She looked around the room for something to give them. 'Wait now and I'll cut you some magnolias from the garden.'

The big magnolia tree grew at the back of the house. Its dark leaves shone in the sun, and the white flowers were like sea-birds high up in the branches. While Mrs Blakiston and Walter stood and watched, Miss Duncaster jumped up to reach the branches. She pulled them down and broke off the creamy flowers, careful not to damage them.

'They go brown so easily,' she explained. She laughed, her

face pink and untidy, as she gave the flowers to Walter. 'He's surprised that I can jump so high,' she said to Mrs Blakiston, laughing again, this time at the boy's face.

'I only jump up like that when I'm really really happy,' said Walter. 'Don't I, Mum? I can jump damn high.'

'What did I hear you say, Walter?'

He had learnt the bad word from his father. 'I can jump as high as the sky,' he said softly.

They walked round to the front of the house. While Mrs Blakiston went to get the gig, Walter waited with Miss Duncaster. He looked around and saw that the brown riding horse was no longer tied to the verandah.

'Where's the horse gone?' he asked.

'What a funny boy you are,' said Miss Duncaster. 'What horse?'

Walter pointed with the magnolias that he was holding. 'It was over by the verandah,' he said. 'We saw it.'

Miss Duncaster bent down and hit him on the arm with her open hand. 'You're damaging the flowers,' she said in a quick, angry voice. 'There was no horse.'

Mrs Blakiston drove up with the gig. 'Come on, Walter. Say goodbye nicely to Miss Duncaster.'

On the way home with his mother Walter said, 'I didn't ask too many questions, did I?'

'No, I don't think so,' said his mother, but she did not sound very sure.

'Then why did she hit me?'

'I don't believe she did. It's just one of your stories.'

■ ■ ■

Walter pointed with the magnolias. 'The horse was over by the verandah,' he said. 'We saw it.'

That evening, when Mr Blakiston came in from the farm for his tea, he saw the big bowl of magnolias in the middle of the table.

'Not ours, are they?' he asked.

'No.' His wife told him of their morning visit to the Duncasters and of Mrs Duncaster's death in the earthquake. While she talked, she picked up pieces of the china vase that had broken in the earthquake and put them together with glue. Walter, his own meal finished, watched her and listened to her talking.

'Of course, it's terrible for Annie, alone in that old house,' he heard her say to his father, 'but she seemed very brave about it.'

'Brave?' Mr Blakiston said. 'She's probably damn pleased about it. For ten years and more she's been shut in that house taking care of that old woman. She'll have a chance to marry now.'

'I don't think she's the kind of woman who gets married.'

'Don't you believe it. I hear more than you do,' said Mr Blakiston.

'Does Joe Sleaver ride a dark brown horse?' Walter asked suddenly.

Mr Blakiston looked surprised. He took his pipe from between his lips and studied it before he answered. 'Yes,' he said, 'I think he does.'

'Walter,' warned Mrs Blakiston, 'you remember what I said to you today, about not asking questions, don't you?'

'I only meant—' began Walter, and stopped.

'What's this about? What are you two talking about?' said Mr Blakiston. 'Why shouldn't Joe Sleaver ride a brown horse if he wants to?'

'Walter thinks that he saw a dark brown horse tied to the Duncasters' verandah this morning,' explained his mother.

'I did see it,' cried Walter. 'Mum saw it too!'

His father and mother looked at each other. Then, with his pipe in his mouth, Mr Blakiston reached forward and picked up a piece of the china vase. 'Well,' he said, smiling as he spoke, 'well, we don't have earthquakes every night.'

'I did see the horse,' Walter said again. Why did his parents want to stop him finding things out? All older people were the same. 'I did see the horse.'

'Of course you saw the damn horse!' said his father suddenly. 'Be quiet about it, that's all.' To his wife he said, more quietly, 'I was thinking yesterday, you know, I shall probably never go back to the Old Country. It's too far away now, too long ago.'

Gathering of the Whakapapa

WITI IHIMAERA

·

Retold by Christine Lindop

*The Māori people of New Zealand have a
long, long history, and at the heart of this is
the whakapapa, the genealogy of families,
which begins in the shadowy past and reaches
forward to the present. The whakapapa lives
not just in books, but also in the memory, and
the names and the stories are chanted aloud
like music.*

*But in this story the books are lost and only
one old, sick man holds the whakapapa in his
memory. It is time to call a favourite grandson
home to help . . .*

The phone rang at work. It was Dad, ringing me in
Wellington from Waituhi, my *whanau*.

'Can you take a week off work?' he asked.

'But Dad!' I answered. 'If I take any more time off, my
boss'll go crazy!'

'It's your Nani Tama,' Dad said. 'He wants you up here,
son.'

'What for now?' I asked.

'Here, you ask him,' Dad said.

The phone went silent, but I could hear Dad saying to
Nani Tama, 'Old man, you're just trouble to him.'

Then Nani Tama's voice called to me.

'Is that you, *mokopuna*?'

'Yes, Nani,' I sighed. 'I'm here.'

'I need you, *mokopuna*. I need you.'

And when I heard his soft voice repeating those words, I knew I would have to go to him.

'All right, Nani.'

'I need you to help me. The work is almost finished now, *mokopuna*. The *whakapapa* is almost done. But I must go to Murupara to finish it. I want you as my driver, not the other fullas. Too fast for me, ay.'

'Don't you worry, Nani. I'll come.'

I went in to see the boss.

He took one look at my face and said, 'Not again!'

'I'm sorry,' I said. 'My grandfather wants me. So I have to go, I just have to.'

■ ■ ■

For some time now, Nani Tama had been busy. After the *whakapapa*, the genealogy of the village, was destroyed, he began to write it all down again.

Before this, the *whakapapa* had been in Nani Tama's old house. It was written in large books and kept in a special cupboard. But then came the night of the fire, the fire that ran through the house and destroyed our past. Everything that we loved was lost: the coats made of feathers, the silver sports cups, the *piupius*, the genealogy, everything except the piece of greenstone, as softly green as the river from where it had come.

In one night, all gone. And Nani Tama, so Dad told me, had gone crazy, looking at the fire and crying out the name of his dead wife, 'Miro! Miro!'

It was a sad time for everyone, but most of all for Nani Tama. He went to stay with his daughter, my Auntie Hiraina, not talking to anyone, trying to find a way out from the ashes of the past.

Much later he had found that way.

'I need a good pen,' he said one morning. 'I need some books to write in. Hurry, I may not have much time.'

He began to write the village genealogy again, to join the past to the present once more. And the village went quiet and listened to his chanting, as he sang the names of the ancestors. Along the lines of the genealogy his voice travelled, searching back, always further back to the first canoes, back across the centuries, joining the past to the present.

His long years of training in *whakapapa* helped him greatly. His memory was like a sharp knife, cutting deep lines into soft wood, finding forgotten routes into the past. And as he chanted, he wrote down the names. Slowly. Carefully. At times he was almost angry with himself at his slowness.

'The memory is working well,' he used to say helplessly, 'but the hands are old and cannot write fast enough.'

So my cousin Timi was chosen to help him. As Nani chanted, Timi wrote down the names.

There were some lines in the genealogy that were difficult to remember. Often Nani Tama's voice suddenly stopped in the middle of a chant. Then the village used to wait in worried silence, wait until, at last, the next name burst out of Nani's mouth. Then the village used to sigh: 'Aaaah, the old man, he remembers . . .'

It took Nani Tama almost a year to write as much as he remembered of the *whakapapa*. During the next year he checked his work, angry when he found a mistake or a line of missing names.

And sometimes while he worked he used to shout:

'*E hara te wa hei haere maku. E hara!*

I cannot go yet. Not yet.'

He was talking to somebody – but there was nobody there.

Now the old man wanted me back home. He wanted me to drive him to Murupara. The gathering of the *whakapapa* was almost done, but it needed one more thing to give our past back to us.

■ ■ ■

'They don't want him to go,' Dad told me. 'Your Nani Tama, he's a sick man. Your Auntie Hiraina says he mustn't do any travelling anywhere.'

We were on our way to Waituhi from the railway station where Dad had met me. Nani Tama wanted to start for Murupara immediately. There was not much time left, he said.

'How sick is he, Dad?' I asked.

Dad did not answer me, but I saw for myself when we arrived at Auntie Hiraina's place.

'Look here, Nani,' I said, 'I'm not taking you nowhere. You hear? You could conk out on me, Nani, and I don't want that to happen.'

He was sitting on the edge of the bed, and he was dressed

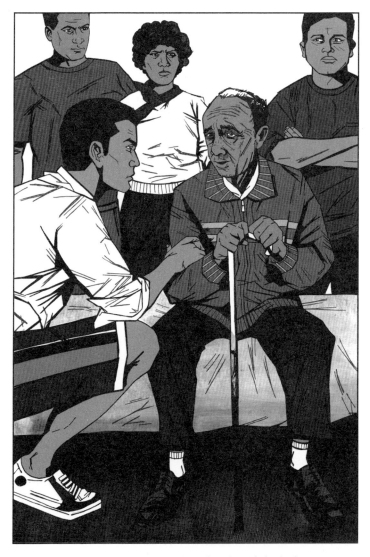

Nani Tama was sitting on the edge of the bed,
and he was dressed to go.

to go. It was a shock to see him; he was so thin and his skin seemed so grey.

'You must take me, *mokopuna*,' he whispered. 'We leave now.'

'And who's going to give you your injections?' shouted Auntie Hiraina. 'You make me wild, Dad!'

Nani Tama looked at each of us – Dad, Auntie Hiraina, my cousin Timi, and myself. His eyes were angry.

'You fullas want me to die here in this room? Looking at these four walls? When the *whakapapa* is not yet finished? Ay, Hiraina? Ay?'

Auntie Hiraina began to cry.

I sighed and touched Nani Tama's face.

'All right, old man,' I said. 'You drive me crazy, you really do. But if you can walk to the door by yourself, without help, I'll take you to Murupara.'

The old man held on tightly to the side of the bed and cried out as he stood up. Every slow, painful step hurt him. But he did it.

'You're really hard on me, *mokopuna*,' he sighed.

I picked him up and carried him to the car. Timi arranged the blankets around him. At the last moment, Auntie Hiraina appeared in her coat, with a small black bag in her hands.

'Well, someone has to give him his injections,' she said.

I started the car.

'Drive carefully, son,' Dad said. 'And bring our grandfather back to us soon.'

■ ■ ■

We travelled all that night, silent most of the time, listening to Nani Tama chanting in the darkness. It was strange to hear him but wonderful too. From time to time he burst into a *waiata* which he had taught Auntie Hiraina. Together they sang, lifting up their voices to send the song flying like a bird through the sky.

We stopped to give Nani his injections, and later to buy some *kai*, and just before midday we arrived at Murupara. A small place. Quiet. Not many people around.

'Who have we come to see, Nani?' I asked.

He looked straight in front of him, unsure.

'Where do we go now?' I asked again.

He did not reply, but he was searching inside himself, staring at the small houses as we drove slowly along the road. Then, at a street corner, he told us to turn. We came to a house with an open door. An old man stood there, waiting.

'We are here, *mokopuna*.'

I stopped the car. The old man came to meet us. He smiled and gently welcomed Nani Tama.

'I have been waiting all night for you. I did not think you would come so late . . .'

In his eyes I saw the message, 'We must hurry.' We carried Nani Tama into the house.

Now that day seems like a dream to me. I remember the two old men sitting at the kitchen table, and the soft sounds of the Māori words as they talked. The noise of the pen as my cousin Timi wrote down the names that Nani Tama repeated to him, all through the quiet afternoon and into the evening. And always the work, the gathering of the *whakapapa*. And the strange feeling that there were other people in the room, people from the past, looking over the shoulders of the two old men, making sure that the work was correct.

Until it was finished. Until it was done.

'You got time for some *kai*?' the old man asked Nani.

Nani Tama did not answer and the old man understood.

'*Haere*, friend,' he whispered.

Crying, they pressed noses to say goodbye, and Auntie Hiraina phoned Waituhi to say we were on our way home.

■ ■ ■

It was early morning and still dark when Waituhi appeared before us. All the lights were on at Auntie Hiraina's place and the village people were waiting for us.

'Huh?' Nani Tama said to them. 'What's wrong with you fullas!'

Many hands reached out to him. He was carried onto the verandah and made comfortable. Smiling, he lifted up the *whakapapa* and offered it to the village. And our hearts were full, because our grandfather had saved our past for us.

He smiled again, our Nani Tama. Then his smile became tired.

'*Na kua tau te wa hei haerenga maku,*' he sighed.

'At last, I may go now.'

And he closed his eyes.

'No, Dad!' Auntie Hiraina cried.

The sun burst across the hills.

*Our hearts were full, because our grandfather
had saved our past for us.*

A Kind of Longing

PHILIP MINCHER

■

Retold by Christine Lindop

Riding a motorbike is a great way to travel. Who cares if the bike is an old Norton or a shiny new Suzuki? It's the speed, the noise of the wind in your ears, the engine roaring under you, burning up the miles. Bikers are free, alone, they go where they want . . .

Free, alone – sometimes lonely. And danger waits at every bend in the road. But for Roy, riding home to Auckland as night falls, it's still a great feeling . . .

Coming up from the river towards the road, Roy looked at his watch. It was half past four. It was cooler now; he could do an hour or two of the journey before dark.

He started off down the road, feeling the heavy fish in the bag against his leg as he walked. He played the fish again in his mind, feeling it pull on the line, fighting him all the way. He walked happily through the afternoon stillness.

A car was parked off the road by the bridge, with three men standing beside it. They watched him coming. They stood drinking from metal cups, looking pleased with themselves, pleased with the wild boar they had shot. It was tied to the roof of their old American car.

They looked at Roy and his fish as he came by.

'Good fishing, then,' one of them said.

'Sure,' Roy said. 'It looks like everybody's got what they came for.'

He stepped into the long grass, found his old Norton, and pushed it up to the road. He felt the men watching him.

'Have a beer,' one of them offered.

'Well, thanks,' Roy said. He took a cup from one of the bags on his bike and went over to the car.

'That's a nice fish,' the man said, filling his cup with beer.

'Not bad,' Roy said. 'He nearly took the fly last night, and I went back to get him today.' He drank his beer.

'He must have a poor memory then,' the man said.

'He just loves Black Gnats,' Roy said, touching the fishing fly pinned to his shirt. They all looked. You could tell that they were not fishermen.

Roy looked at the dead boar with its long dangerous teeth.

'Big one,' he said, and finished the beer.

The guy offered the bottle.

'No, thanks. I've got to get going.'

He walked back to the bike and went on packing. The men stood around with their beer, watching him. Roy picked up the fish and held it up to show them how big it was, and they smiled. He packed it away in one of the bags. He sat down on the grass and pulled on his boots, thinking that it hadn't been a bad weekend. He felt the men watching him. They were friendly, but there was something about it, a kind of feeling he wasn't sure about.

He put on his crash helmet and his gloves. Then he started the bike and waved goodbye. The men smiled, and one of them lifted his beer for good luck. 'I'm on my own,' Roy thought. 'That's what it is. They're three friends out together in the afternoon, and I'm on my own, with two hundred miles to go. It's a small thing, but that's what it is, all right.'

He turned away and rode the Norton down the road.

■   ■   ■

The road stayed near the river for the next eight or ten miles. Sometimes the rocky walls of the valley hid the river, and sometimes you could see it far below you. In places road and river went side by side, and you could see the wet rocks shining in the late afternoon sun, and the deep black water at the bends. It was always good to be close to a river, Roy thought. Next time he would fish down river from the bridge.

The road turned away from the river at last, and joined the highway. Roy let the bike go faster. He felt the old feeling coming as the miles went by. All the things that hurt disappeared, all the things that didn't matter. He didn't need to think, not about being alone, not about anything.

He did sixty-five miles in the first hour. He felt calm and easy. Sometimes it worried him, riding fast, but this afternoon was fine. When it was dark, he would slow down.

He rode on past the rich farmland. He thought about the farmers, finishing work, perhaps having their tea. That made him feel a little hungry. Maybe about halfway he would stop for a cup of coffee and something to eat.

He came round a bend and saw a car just disappearing round the next bend. He slowed down a little, waiting for a place to pass it. It was a big, old car, and as he came up behind it, the driver speeded up and went fast into the next bend. Roy stayed behind him, waiting for a straight piece of road. Maybe the guy just didn't like bikes.

The place came at last, half a mile of straight empty road, going up a small hill. He checked his mirror, and passed the car. He went up the hill, leaving the car behind, and he was alone again on a straight road. And then the world exploded underneath him!

It came with a sudden crash, like a shot from a gun behind him. A moment later he realized what it was – he was riding a flying machine on a back tyre in pieces, fighting wildly to stay on and to slow the Norton down from sixty-five to zero. The big bike flew from one side of the road to the other, but as it went up the hill, it began to go slower. Then a car was coming and he was off the road, and at last the bike ran hard against a bank and stopped.

Roy turned off the engine and sat back. Then the car he had passed came up and stopped beside him. An unpleasant face stared at him from the front passenger seat.

'Bad luck!'

The voice sounded pleased. Somebody laughed. Then the old car roared away and disappeared over the hill.

Roy got off the bike. He was shaking just a little. He decided not to think about the guys in the car for a while. He wanted to calm down first. He looked down the road, half a mile of it, straight with no ditch, and he felt how lucky he had been: *A long straight road and no ditch, man . . .*

He turned and looked up the road. There was a house near the top of the hill. He half walked, half rode the bike to the

At last the bike ran hard against a bank and stopped.
Roy turned off the engine and sat back.

farm gate. They would let him leave his bike there, surely. He stopped by the back door and turned off the engine.

A big man in jeans, with only socks on his feet, came to the door. Roy felt the farmer looking at him, deciding about him while he explained.

'On your own?'

'Yes.'

'Just a minute,' the farmer said, and got his boots.

They put the bike in one of the farm buildings, and Roy felt better about it.

'Lucky it happened there,' the farmer said.

'That's true,' said Roy. 'And lucky it was the back wheel.'

'I used to have one of these things,' the farmer said, and he reached over to hold the bike. He seemed to be looking back in time. 'It'll be safe here,' he said.

Roy took out the fish and gave it to him.

'Well, he's a big one!' said the farmer. 'We'll keep him for you.'

'No,' Roy said. 'Give him to the cook. Do you think I'll get a ride this time of day?'

'Easy,' the farmer said. 'One of those cattle trucks is what you need – take you all the way to Westfield.'

'Thanks again,' Roy said, and walked back up to the road.

It was nearly dark. He took his gloves and put his crash helmet on. 'Then people will see I'm not just out walking,' he thought. That was what he thought at the beginning.

■ ■ ■

The first two or three cars did not matter. But then he knew he had a long walk in front of him. Most people did not even slow down before they decided not to take him. He was halfway up the second long hill, and it was quite dark, when he heard the first cattle truck.

He waited as the big truck came closer. Then he saw the driver's face looking at him, and he remembered it when the truck had gone. It wasn't unfriendly, he thought – the guy just didn't care. He watched the truck go slowly up the hill.

He started to walk again. He felt a kind of loneliness walking in the dark. It was the way the truck driver had looked at him. The guy just didn't care. Or maybe he didn't want a stranger with him all that way. Maybe he just didn't want to talk.

More cars passed, but he didn't even try asking for a ride any more. He walked on, not caring, knowing how alone in the world he was.

He had walked perhaps another five miles when he heard his favourite sound. A bike came up fast behind him, and went round the next corner. Roy heard it slow down, turn and come back. The rider stopped and waited for Roy.

It was a big modern bike, Japanese, he guessed. The rider sat looking back at him, crash helmet shining. Roy was next to the bike before he realized that the rider was a girl – a tall, leggy girl in jeans and boots, and perhaps there was fair hair under the helmet. Roy stared as they spoke.

'Which way you going, mister?'

'Auckland.'

'That makes two of us. You have a crash?'

'Tyre went.'

'No fun.'

Roy felt her eyes watching him as she spoke.

'Well,' she said, 'talking about it won't get us home.'

'Sure,' said Roy. His ears were getting hot under his crash helmet. He climbed up behind her and they were off.

She rode fast from the beginning. This was a real bike and a real rider. Roy felt good about it – good to be on wheels again, good that somebody cared enough to stop.

Close to his face the girl asked, 'What kind of bike, mister?'

'Norton. 500cc.'

'Front wheel or back?'

'Back.'

'Not so bad,' she said. 'Better back than front, any day.'

'Sure,' Roy said. He wanted to talk to this girl, but he could not get the words out.

They rode on in silence in the dark. She knew about bikes all right. 'With a guy it's easy,' Roy thought. 'You have a crash, you get a ride, you climb on the bike. You don't even notice that he can ride it well. But this is a girl and she knows what she's doing. That doesn't mean you can't talk to her,' he told himself. 'You've seen girls before, man.'

Her voice came back to him: 'Where have you come from, mister?'

'Pukatea Valley.'

'Yes? How was the fishing?'

'Not bad,' Roy said, before he had time to wonder at her question.

'Nice water by the old bridge. What were they taking?'

'Black Gnat,' he said, and there was more than wonder. He felt that hot pain behind his eyes.

'Wet or dry?'

'Wet,' said Roy, and his voice shook a little with the wonder of it. And in his heart he felt an ache that came from a kind of longing. This was the girl he had been longing for all his life – a tall, leggy girl who rode a 750cc Suzuki and knew about fly-fishing.

For a while they rode and did not speak. Then, back on straight road, the girl said, close to his face, 'My brother caught a six-pound fish under that bridge one year.'

'Really!' Roy was beginning to understand. 'How long ago was that?'

'Maybe five years ago. Ross played him for half an hour before he pulled him in.'

'Sounds like he's a good fisherman, your brother,' Roy said.

'He was,' she said, and that was all.

And Roy, guessing what she meant, knew it was not the kind of thing you could shout about above the noise of the wind and the engine.

After a few miles the girl said, 'My name's Kay, mister.'

Roy said his own name. It sounded strange to him.

'Well, Roy, you going to buy me a cup of coffee when we get to the next town?'

'Sure,' Roy said. 'Sure thing, Kay.'

They dropped their speed and rode into the town. It was quiet on a Sunday evening. They found the place they wanted, and got off the bike.

Her hair was long and fair and blown about by the wind. In the coffee shop he saw her face for the first time, and he

*They sat drinking their coffee, watching and listening,
getting the idea of each other.*

felt that kind of longing from way back, and he sat down beside her, knowing what it was.

'How long were you walking back there?' Her voice was soft and pleasant after the shouted conversation on the road.

'Perhaps five or six miles,' Roy said. 'Nobody was interested.'

'They never are.'

'It's not the kind of thing you worry about,' he said.

'No.' They sat drinking their coffee, watching and listening, getting the idea of each other.

'You go fishing a lot?' she said.

'Sure. Fishing. Moving around.'

'Always travel alone?'

'My friend got killed,' Roy said. It came out like that. There was not much else that he could say. He felt a kind of softness in her eyes that took him by the heart.

'What about you?' he said.

'What about me?'

'I mean, you can tell me about your brother.' He saw her eyes – their softness, the quiet hurt as his words hit her.

'Ross got killed in the army,' she said. 'It was his first week – just a stupid accident. He was only twenty. He fell off the back of a truck and hit his head. He used to do wild, crazy things all the time – but then what killed him was just a stupid accident . . .'

He played with his spoon in the coffee.

'What about your friend?' she asked after a while.

'Plane,' Roy said. 'Another thing that just couldn't happen.'

He saw it in his mind – the broken plane, that moment he

could never forget for the rest of his life. This was something they both knew, he and this girl: a death that you couldn't believe. And that feeling was always with you, everywhere, like a voice that whispers in your ear, 'There will never be enough road any more, enough water, enough air . . .'

But beyond the feelings of hurt, old and new, he knew that they were telling each other the truth about themselves, not hiding things. Was he choosing the right words? It didn't matter. Now he asked, 'Where've you been today then, on your big bike?'

'Tauranga.'

'Stay the weekend?'

'Down this morning. It's only two hundred and sixty miles there and back,' she said. 'My father's in a kind of hospital down there. I don't stay because one visit each time is all I can do.'

'I'm sorry,' Roy said.

It was all in her eyes. In his mind Roy saw a strong man broken – the father who would never get old, never die. How could you believe it, live with it?

Maybe he taught them to fish, Roy thought, this girl and her brother, dead at twenty from his accident. Maybe he taught them all those good things and they all had fun together, and then suddenly she looked around and she was the only one left. Maybe that's why she rides the big bike.

The time was starting to get heavy now.

'What do you say we get on the road?' Kay said.

'Sure.'

They went out and Roy felt the heaviness going. It was all

right if you knew when to get up and go. They put on their crash helmets and the tall leggy girl started her bike. Roy climbed on behind her, and they went away laughing. They rode gently out of the sleepy town; then they reached the highway and the bike roared away into the night.

Roy felt all right about riding on the back. Sometimes, if you weren't sure about the rider, you weren't happy when he went fast, but this girl was okay. They rode, not talking, enjoying the night ride on their big fast machine. Roy thought about the things they were passing – the cattle in the fields, the night sounds of the farms. Lights appeared and cars sped past, and he thought about all the people going places. He felt Kay close to him, with her long friendly shoulders and her fair hair flying back from under her helmet. He could go on and on. He didn't care about the people who hated you before they saw you, or enjoyed watching you in trouble on the road, or let you walk because they didn't want to think about you. He felt that none of it could touch him now, or ever, that all the hurt had gone, and the shock from the deaths of friends and the bad feelings that came from people's unkind words.

A notice warned of bends in the road, and Kay cut their speed, and they rode the big bike down into the first bend.

Cars came up from down below, their lights showing the narrow road and the banks on each side. Most of the cars seemed to be in too much of a hurry, Roy thought.

They reached the bottom of the narrow valley, where he knew the river ran close to the road. He thought about that clear mountain water among the trees. Then they started to climb. They rode up the hill and into the first bend. And death came down to meet them on the wrong side of the road.

The lights of the car were right in front of them. They had nowhere to go, and not enough time to hate the guy who was killing them. Roy put his arms round Kay. He felt his face against her shoulder, their helmets close together. Then they were off the road and into the ditch as the car went past, moving too late to its own side of the road. They went on and on, fighting the ditch, crashing into the bank, and then they were over the bank and sailing, a moment's space before the hurt that was coming. They crashed down the bank, and Roy held tight to Kay, and they were off the bike and dying together, and the ground came up to knock the life out of his body, and he reached for Kay as he fell. Impossibly, he was still alive, but as he fell, crashed, broke, he didn't care – he only reached for Kay, longed for her.

He came to rest; there was a taste of blood and a whisper of pain through the shock, and he felt cold water around him. He lay in the icy water of the ditch, and knew he was still alive. Then he was moving along the ditch on hands and knees, searching for Kay through the pain and shock.

He pulled himself along the ditch until he found her. She was lying face down. He touched her, and turned her over as gently as he could.

Time had stopped. It was like a bad dream, made of all the deaths that had gone before. He said her name, and it came thick and strange through his painful lips. She looked at him and he waited for an impossible moment, and then

They rode up the hill and into the first bend. And death came down to meet them on the wrong side of the road.

she began to cry as the shock hit her, and that was all the hope he needed.

He took off her helmet, and gently pushed her hair back, and somewhere above them he heard voices and a crashing sound as help came. The pain in his legs began to come alive. He put his arm around Kay, loving the life that returned as she cried, life and pain coming together. And that was all the hope he needed. He guessed it must be all the hope in the world.

Because, for all the time that it lasted, they would have it together.

The Silk

JOY COWLEY

■

Retold by Christine Lindop

It came from China, a piece of blue silk that lit up the room with its colours – the peacocks with their shining silvery tails, the blue lakes and the white waterfalls, the cloudy mountains and the dark blue trees. It was too lovely to wear, too beautiful to cut with scissors.

All through the long years of a marriage the silk had stayed safely in its box – waiting, but not forgotten. And now the time had come . . .

When Mr Blackie became ill again that autumn, both he and Mrs Blackie knew that it was for the last time. For many weeks neither spoke of it; but the understanding was in their eyes as they watched each other through the days and nights. It was a look seen in the faces of the old and the very young, neither sad, nor hopeless, just a quiet understanding; they accepted what was coming.

It showed in other ways too. There were no more cross words from Mrs Blackie about her lazy old husband. Instead she took care of him day and night. She managed their money carefully to buy him his favourite foods; she let the district nurse visit him, but no more than twice a week.

Mr Blackie went to his bed and stayed there quietly. He had never talked much about the past, but now he spoke a lot about their earlier days. Sometimes, to Mrs Blackie's surprise, he remembered things that she had forgotten. He talked very little about the present, and never in those weeks about the future.

Then, on the first icy morning of the winter, while Mrs Blackie was filling his hot water bottle, he sat up in bed to see out the window. He could see a row of houses outside, with ice on the grass in front of them, like a white carpet.

'The ground will be hard,' he said at last. 'Hard as a rock.'

Mrs Blackie looked up quickly. 'Not yet,' she said.

'Soon, I think.' He smiled, but she knew he was saying sorry to her. She put the hot water bottle into its cover.

'Lie down or you'll catch cold,' she said.

He lay back against the pillow, but as she moved about him, putting the hot water bottle at his feet, he stared at the shapes of ice on the window.

'Amy, you'll get a double plot, won't you?' he said. 'I won't rest easy if I think that one day you're going to sleep by someone else.'

'What a thing to say!' The corners of her mouth moved suddenly. 'You know very well I won't do that.'

'It was your idea to buy single beds,' he said crossly.

'Oh, Herb—' She looked at the window, away again. 'We'll have a double plot.' For a second or two she waited by his bed, then she sat down beside his feet, with one hand resting on top of the other. This was the way that she always sat when she had something important to say.

'You know, I've been thinking on and off about the silk.'

'The silk?' He turned his head towards her.

'I want to use it for your laying-out pyjamas.'

'No, Amy,' he said. 'Not the silk. That was your wedding present, the only thing that I brought back with me.'

'What am I going to do with it now?' she said. When he didn't answer, she got up, opened the cupboard door and took down the wooden box. 'All these years we've kept it. We should use it some time.'

'Not on me,' he said.

'I've been thinking about your pyjamas.' She fitted a key into the lock on the box. 'It'll be just right.'

'It'll be a right mistake, I think,' he said. But he could not keep the excitement out of his voice. He watched her hands as she opened the box, and pulled back the sheets of thin white paper. Below them lay the blue of the silk. They were both silent as she took it out and put it on the bed.

'Makes the whole room look different, doesn't it?' he said. 'I nearly forgot it looked like this.' His hands moved with difficulty across the bed cover. Gently she picked up the blue silk and let it fall in a river over his fingers.

'Aah,' he sighed, bringing it close to his eyes. 'All the way from China.' He smiled. 'I kept it on me all the time. You know that, Amy? There were people on that ship who wanted to steal that silk. But I kept it pinned round my middle.'

'You told me,' she said.

He held the silk against his face. 'It's the birds that you notice,' he said.

'At first,' said Mrs Blackie. She ran her finger over one of the peacocks that marched across the land of silk. They were

'Aah,' Mr Blackie sighed, bringing the silk close to his eyes.
'All the way from China.'

beautiful birds, shining blue, with silver threads in their tails. 'I used to like them best, but after a while you see much more, just as fine, only smaller.' She pushed her glasses higher up her nose and looked closely at the silk, her eyes following her finger. She saw islands with waterfalls between little houses and dark blue trees; flat lakes with small fishing boats; mountains with their tops in silvery clouds; and back again to a peacock with one foot in the air above a rock.

'They just don't make anything as beautiful as this in this country,' she said.

Mr Blackie held up the box, enjoying the smell of the wood. 'Don't cut it, Amy. It's too good for someone like me.' But his eyes were asking her to disagree with him.

'I'll get the pattern tomorrow,' she said.

The next day, while the district nurse was giving him his injection, she went down to the store and chose a pattern from the pattern books. Mr Blackie, who had worn boring pyjamas all his life, looked at the picture of the young man on the front of the packet and crossed his arms.

'What's this – a Chinese suit? That's young men's clothes, not suitable for me,' he said.

'Rubbish,' said Mrs Blackie.

'Modern rubbish,' he said, 'that's what it is. You're never putting those on me.'

'It's not your job to decide,' said Mrs Blackie.

'Not my job? I'll get up and fight – you wait and see.'

'All right, Herb, if you really don't like it—'

But now he had won, he was happy. 'Oh, go on, Amy. It's not such a bad idea. In fact, I think they're fine. It's that nurse, you see. The injection hurt.' He looked at the pattern. 'When do you start?'

'Well—'

'This afternoon?'

'I could pin the pattern out after lunch, I suppose.'

'Do it in here,' he said. 'Bring in your machine and pins and things so I can watch.'

She turned her head and looked at him. 'I'm not using the machine,' she said. 'I'm doing it all by hand – every thread of it. My eyes aren't as good as they were, but nobody in this world can say that I'm not still good with my needle.'

His eyes closed as he thought. 'How long?'

'Eh?'

'Until it's finished.'

She turned the pattern over in her hands. 'Oh – about three or four weeks. That is – if I work hard.'

'No,' he said. 'Too long.'

'Oh, Herb, you want me to do a good job, don't you?' she said.

'Amy—' He shook his head on the pillow.

'I can use the machine for some of it,' she said, in a quieter voice.

'How long?'

'A week,' she whispered.

Although the doctor had told him to lie flat in bed, he made her give him another pillow that afternoon. She took the pillow from her own bed, shook it, and put it behind his neck. Then she measured his body, legs, and arms.

'I'll have to make them a bit smaller,' she said, writing

down big black numbers. Mr Blackie was waiting, his eyes wide. He looked brighter, she thought, than he had for weeks.

As she arranged the silk on her bed and started pinning the first of the pattern pieces, he described the journey home by boat, the stop at Hong Kong, and the man who had sold him the silk.

'Most of it was rubbish,' he said. 'This was the only good thing that he had, and I still paid too much for it. You got to argue with these people, they told me. But there were others who wanted that silk, and I had to buy it – or lose it.' He looked at her hands. 'What are you doing now? You just put that bit down.'

'It wasn't right,' she said, through lips closed on pins. 'It needs to be in just the right place. I have to join a tree to a tree, not to the middle of a waterfall.'

She lifted the pattern pieces many times before everything was right. Then it was evening, and Mr Blackie could talk no more. He lay back on his pillows, his eyes red from tiredness.

'Go to sleep,' she said. 'Enough's enough for one day.'

'I want you to cut it out first,' he said.

'Let's leave it until the morning,' she said, and they both knew that she did not want to put the scissors to the silk.

'Tonight,' he said.

'I'll make the tea first.'

'After,' he said.

She picked up the scissors and held them for a moment. Then together they felt the pain as the scissors closed cleanly in that first cut. The silk would never again be the same. They were changing it, arranging the pattern of some fifty years to make something new and different. When she had cut out the first piece, she held it up, still pinned to the paper, and said, 'The back of the top.' Then she put it down and went on as quickly as she could, because she knew that he would not rest until she had finished.

One by one the pieces left the body of silk. Each time the scissors moved, mountains fell in half, peacocks were cut from head to tail. In the end, there was nothing on the bed but a few shining threads. Mrs Blackie picked them up and put them back in the wooden box. Then she took her pillow from Mr Blackie's bed and made him comfortable before she went into the kitchen to make the tea.

He was very tired the next morning, but refused to sleep while she was working with the silk. From time to time she thought of a reason to leave the room. He slept then, but never for long. After no more than half an hour, he would call. She would find him awake, waiting for her to start again.

In that day and the next, she did all the machine work. It was a long, boring job, because first she sewed all the pieces in place by hand. Mr Blackie silently watched every move she made. Sometimes she saw him studying the silk, and on his face was a look that she remembered. It was the way that he had looked at her when they were young lovers. That hurt a little. He didn't care about the silk more than he cared about her, she knew that, but he saw something in it that she didn't. She never asked him what it was.

Someone of her age did not question these things or ask for explanations. She just went on with the work, thinking only of the sewing and the silk.

On the Friday afternoon, four days after she'd started the pyjamas, she finished the buttonholes and sewed on the buttons. She had had to work more quickly at the end. In the four days Mr Blackie had become weaker. She knew that when the pyjamas were finished and put back in the box, he would be more interested in food and rest.

She cut the last thread and put away the needle.

'That's it, Herb,' she said, showing him her work.

He tried to lift his head. 'Bring them over here,' he said.

'Well – what do you think?' As she brought the pyjamas closer, he saw them clearly and he smiled.

'Try them on?' he said.

She shook her head. 'I measured you carefully,' she said. 'They'll fit.'

'We should make sure,' he said.

Why didn't she want him to try them on? She couldn't find a reason. 'All right,' she said, turning on the heater. 'Just to make sure the buttons are right.'

She took off his thick pyjamas and put on the silk. She stepped back to look at him.

'Well, I have to say that's a fine job. I could move the top button a little bit, but really they fit beautifully.'

He smiled at her. 'Light, aren't they?' He looked all down his body and moved his toes. 'All the way from China. I kept it with me day and night. Know that, Amy?'

'Do you like them?'

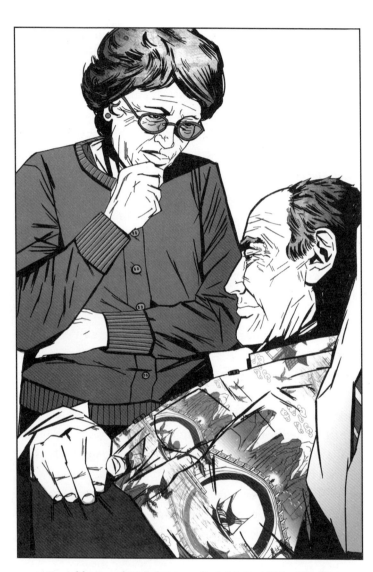

'I could move the top button a little bit,' said Mrs Blackie,
'but really they fit beautifully.'

He tried not to look too pleased. 'All right. A little bit small.'

'They are not, and you know it,' Mrs Blackie said crossly. 'It wouldn't hurt to say thank you. Here, put your hands down and I'll change you before you get cold.'

He crossed his arms. 'You did a really good job, Amy. Think I'll keep them on for a bit.'

'No.' She picked up his thick pyjamas.

'Why not?'

'Because you can't,' she said. 'It – it's not the right thing to do. And the nurse will be here soon.'

'Oh, you and your ideas.' He was too weak to stop her, but as she changed him, he still could not take his eyes away from the silk. 'Wonder who made it?'

She didn't answer, but a picture came to her of a Chinese woman sitting at a machine making silk. She was dressed in beautiful Eastern clothes, and although she had Eastern eyes, she looked like Mrs Blackie.

'Do you think there are places like that?' Mr Blackie asked.

She picked the pyjamas up quickly and put them in the box. 'You're the one who's been to the East,' she said. 'Now get some rest or you'll be tired when the nurse arrives.'

The district nurse did not come that afternoon. Nor in the evening. It was half-past three the next morning when Mrs Blackie heard the nurse's footsteps, and the doctor's, outside the house.

She was in the kitchen, waiting. She sat with straight back and dry eyes, with one hand resting on top of the other.

'Mrs Blackie, I'm sorry—'

She didn't answer and turned to the doctor. 'He didn't say goodbye,' she said, her voice angry. 'Just before I phoned. His hand was over the side of the bed. I touched it. It was cold.'

The doctor nodded.

'No sound of any kind,' she said. 'He was fine last night.'

Again the doctor nodded. He put his hand on her shoulder for a moment, then went into the bedroom. A minute later he returned, closing his bag, speaking kindly.

Mrs Blackie sat still, hearing words. Peacefully. Brave. The words dropped onto her. They didn't seem to mean anything.

'He didn't say goodbye.' She shook her head. 'Not a word.'

'But look, Mrs Blackie,' the nurse said gently. 'It was going to happen. You know that. He was—'

'I know, I know.' She turned away crossly. Why didn't they understand? 'I just wanted him to say goodbye. That's all.'

The doctor offered her something to help her sleep but she pushed it away. And she refused the cup of tea that the district nurse put in front of her. When they picked up their bags and went towards the bedroom, she followed them.

'In a few minutes,' the doctor said. 'If you'll leave us—'

'I'm getting his pyjamas,' she said. 'I need to change a button. I can do it now.'

When she entered the room, she looked at Mr Blackie's bed and saw that the doctor had pulled up the sheet. Quickly, she lifted the wooden box, took a needle, thread, scissors, her glasses, and went back to the kitchen. Through the door

*Trees moved above the water, peacocks danced with white fire
in their tails. And the little bridges . . .*

she heard the nurse's voice, 'Poor old thing,' and she knew that they were not talking about her.

She sat down at the table to thread the needle. Her eyes were clear, but for a long time her hands refused to obey her. At last, her needle and thread ready, she opened the wooden box. The beauty of the silk always surprised her. As she arranged the pyjamas on the table, she was filled with a strong, warm feeling, the first good feeling that she had had that morning. The silk was real. The light above the table filled everything with life. Trees moved above the water, peacocks danced with white fire in their tails. And the little bridges . . .

Mrs Blackie took off her glasses, cleaned them, put them on again. She sat down and touched one bridge with her finger, then another. And another. She turned over the pyjama coat and looked carefully at the back. It was there, on every bridge; something she hadn't noticed before. She got up and fetched her magnifying glass.

As the bridge in the pattern on the silk grew, the little group of threads, which had been no bigger than a grain of rice, became a man.

Mrs Blackie forgot about the button, and the quiet voices in the bedroom. She brought the magnifying glass nearer her eyes.

It was a man, and he was standing with one arm held out on the highest part of the bridge between two islands. Mrs Blackie studied him for a long time, then she sat up and smiled. Yes, he was waving. Or perhaps, she thought, he was calling her to join him.

GLOSSARY

ancestor   a person in your family who lived a long time ago

ashes   what is left after something has been destroyed by burning

ay (*New Zealand English*)   something you say when you want somebody to agree with you, or reply to what you have said

bank   a higher piece of ground at the edge of a road, a field, etc.

Bible   the holy book of the Christian religion

boar   a wild pig

brick   a hard block of clay used for building

burst   to come from somewhere suddenly

buttonhole   a hole on a piece of clothing for a button to be put through

candle   a round stick of wax which gives light when it burns

canoe   a long narrow boat which you move along in the water with paddles

cattle truck   a large vehicle used for carrying cows

cc (**cubic centimetres**)   a way of measuring the size of an engine in a car or motorbike

chant   to sing or say something using only a few notes that are repeated many times

china   a fine white clay; cups, plates, etc. made out of this

colonial (*n & adj*)   a person who lives in a colony and who comes from the country that controls the colony

conk out (*New Zealand English*)   to stop working

creamy   of a pale yellowish-white colour

crest   a design used as the symbol of a family with a long history

damn (*adj*) (*informal*)   used to describe something or someone you do not like, or to emphasize what you are saying

district nurse   a nurse who visits people in their homes

ditch   a long channel at the side of a road that takes away water

earthquake a sudden strong shaking of the ground

feather one of the soft light parts that cover a bird's body

fly *(n)* something that looks like a fly that is put on a hook and
used to catch fish

fullas (*New Zealand English*) a group of people

gathering bringing things together into one place

genealogy the record of a family's history

gig a small light carriage pulled by a horse

gloves something you wear to keep your hands warm

glue something sticky that is used for joining things together

guy (*informal*) a man

helmet a kind of hard hat worn to protect the head

highway a main road for travelling long distances

injection putting a drug into someone's body with a needle

laying-out pyjamas pyjamas (a loose jacket and trousers worn to
sleep in) that are put on a dead body before it is buried

longing a strong feeling of wanting something

magnifying glass a round piece of glass that you hold and look
through that makes things look bigger than they really are

memory the ability to remember things

needle a small sharp piece of steel used for sewing, with a hole
for thread at one end

nod to move your head up and down to show agreement

peacock a large bird with a long blue and green tail

pillow a soft thing you put your head on when you are in bed

pin (*v & n*) a short piece of metal with a sharp point, used for
holding pieces of cloth together when sewing

plot a small piece of land used for a special purpose

roar to make a very loud, deep sound

shock a strong feeling of surprise when something unpleasant
happens

sigh to let out a long deep breath to show you are sad, tired, etc.

silk a kind of fine smooth cloth that is made from the threads of an insect called a silkworm

slow down to move at a slower speed

speed how fast something is moving; **speed up** to move faster

store a shop that sells a lot of different kinds of things

thread a thin string of cotton used for sewing

tyre a thick rubber ring that fits around the edge of a wheel

vase a container made of glass, china, etc. used for holding flowers

MĀORI WORDS USED IN THE STORY

haere goodbye

kai food

mokopuna grandchild

nani grandfather

piupiu a skirt of leaves

waiata a song or chant

whanau family

ACTIVITIES

Before Reading

Before you read the stories, read the introductions at the beginning, then use these activities to help you think about the stories. How much can you guess or predict?

1 *After the Earthquake* (story introduction page 1). Do you agree (A) or disagree (D) with these ideas?

In small towns . . .
1 . . . it is hard to keep a secret.
2 . . . people talk about each other too much.
3 . . . people usually help each other when there are problems.

Children . . .
4 . . . should always hear the truth from adults.
5 . . . should never ask personal questions.
6 . . . usually know when adults are not being honest with them.

2 *Gathering of the Whakapapa* (story introduction page 17). What do you think about these ideas? Choose words to complete the sentences.

1 It is *important* / *not important* to know your family history.
2 Most people *know* / *do not know* the names of people in their family further back than their grandparents.

3 In the future people will be *more* / *less* interested in their family history.

4 *Writing stories down* / *Chanting stories aloud* is the best way to remember them.

5 You must always help your *family* / *friends* if they ask you.

3 *A Kind of Longing* (story introduction page 27). What can you guess about this story? Choose one or more of these ideas.

1 Roy's bike breaks down.

2 Roy's bike goes off the road.

3 Roy gives someone a lift.

4 Someone gives Roy a lift.

5 Roy meets someone unpleasant.

6 Roy meets someone nice.

7 Roy is hurt.

8 Roy gets home safely.

4 *The Silk* (story introduction page 43). Which words do you think will be in the story? Choose one word from each group.

1 knife   edge   scissors

2 nail   pin   glue

3 sew   mend   cover

4 pyjamas   skirt   trousers

5 string   thread   rope

6 fork   wheel   needle

7 picture   shape   pattern

8 button   zip   key

ACTIVITIES

After Reading

1 In *After the Earthquake* perhaps Mr and Mrs Blakiston talked about Miss Duncaster and the horse after Walter had gone to bed. Put their conversation in the right order and write in the speakers' names. Mr Blakiston speaks first (number 4).

1 _____ 'So while you were going in the front door, Joe Sleaver was going out the back door!'

2 _____ 'Yes, he's always asking questions. Too many, sometimes. But when we arrived, I did ask Miss Duncaster if she had a visitor.'

3 _____ 'You're right, I suppose. Still, I wonder – Bill Gabriel has a brown horse . . .'

4 _____ 'So Walter noticed the horse. I'm not surprised. He always wants to know what's going on.'

5 _____ 'Shhh! Walter will hear you. We don't *know* it was Joe's horse. And perhaps he just called to say he was sorry about her mother.'

6 _____ 'She said there was nobody there!'

7 _____ 'Really, it's not right to talk about these things. Her mother has just died.'

8 _____ 'And what did she say to that?'

9 _____ 'Then why didn't she say so? I think she had something to hide.'

2 In *Gathering of the Whakapapa*, the grandson writes to his boss to explain why he cannot return to work yet. Use these words to complete his letter (one word for each gap).

after / back / dear / eyes / genealogy / grandfather / help / hope / need / ready / sorry / successful / work / yours

_____ Mr Reynolds, I am _____ to tell you that I will _____ to be away from _____ for another week. Yesterday I returned from Murupara, where I took my _____ to complete the _____. The visit was _____, but just _____ he had given the books of the whakapapa to the village, he closed his _____ and died. Now we are all getting _____ to say goodbye to him, and I have to stay to _____ my father and the rest of the family. I _____ to be _____ in the office by the 25th.

   _____ truly, George Nepia

3 What happens next to Roy and Kay? Read about this story in *About the Authors* on page 68. Imagine a moment in Roy and Kay's 'brief and wonderful time', and write a short paragraph about it. Use these ideas to help you.

- Roy visits Kay in hospital / falls in love / at last Kay gets better / afraid to ride bike again / Roy helps her
- Roy and Kay go fishing (same place as before) / don't catch any fish / not important / a great day
- A day in the mountains / talking about why they like biking / talking about each other
- A camping weekend together / by a wild and beautiful river / under the stars / Roy asks Kay to marry him

4 Here is a conversation between Amy and Herb Blackie about the silk. Choose one suitable word to fill each gap.

HERB: I've got a _____ for you, Amy. I _____ it in Hong Kong. Lots of _____ wanted it, you know, so I had to keep it _____ round my _____ all the way _____.

AMY: Oh, Herb, it's _____! Look at these _____ with their long _____. And the little _____ on the lake here, look. And the _____ is really beautiful, isn't it?

HERB: It's the same blue _____ your eyes.

AMY: Oh, Herb, you know that's not _____! But it's _____, and thank you _____ much. I'm going to put it _____ safely and keep it for something really _____.

5 Use the clues to complete the crossword with words from the stories.

1 A hard hat that keeps your head safe.
2 A very bad surprise.
3 A small thin piece of metal with a point at one end, used to keep material in place when sewing.
4 Things you wear on your hands to keep them warm.

5 To let out a deep breath because you are sad or tired.
6 A raised piece of land at the side of a road.
7 An informal word for a man.

What is the eighth word, hidden in the crossword?
Which character, in which story, feels this, and why?

6 **Here are the thoughts of four characters (one from each story).**
   Who is thinking, which story is it, and what has just happened
   in the story?

   1 'I didn't mean to tell him about Ross, and Dad. It just
      came out. But I didn't have to explain anything – he just
      understood. He knows what it's like. He seems like a really
      nice guy. And he likes fishing . . .'

   2 'It's strange, but I knew he was coming. I knew all night.
      And he came just in time. Sometimes today I thought there
      was too much to do, and we wouldn't finish the work.
      But we did. And now he's gone. Dear friend! His time is
      coming. I know I will not see him again . . .'

   3 'That awful child! Asking questions about things that
      are none of his business! He should learn to keep quiet.
      It's lucky his mother had gone to get their gig. I hope she
      didn't see me . . .'

   4 'Poor woman. What's she going to do without him? For
      months he's been the centre of her life. She's been thinking
      about him and taking care of him, night and day. Even now
      she wants to change a button on his pyjamas. I'll make her
      another cup of tea in a minute . . .'

7 **Death can bring change and hope as well as sadness. In which stories do these things happen? Discuss your answers.**

   1 Death brings people closer together.
   2 Death gives people the chance to show their love.
   3 Death gives someone a new chance in life.
   4 Death comes at the right time, bringing rest.

8 **Here is a short poem (a kind of poem called a haiku) about one of the stories. Which of the four stories is it about?**

> *Mountains, lakes, peacocks –*
> *a message comes from beyond*
> *to the one who waits.*

Here is another haiku, about the same story.

> *From a distant land*
> *a husband calls his dear wife:*
> *Join me! Come to me!*

A haiku is a Japanese poem, which is always in three lines, and the three lines always have 5, 7, and 5 syllables each, like this:

| From | a | dis | tant | land | = 5 syllables
| a | hus | band | calls | his | dear | wife   = 7 syllables
| Join | me! | Come | to | me! | = 5 syllables

Now write your own haiku, one for each of the other three stories. Think about what each story is really about. What are the important ideas for you? Remember to keep to three lines of 5, 7, 5 syllables each.

ABOUT THE AUTHORS

JAMES COURAGE

James Courage (1903–1963) was born in Christchurch, New Zealand, and grew up on his father's sheep farm. As a young man he went to England to study at Oxford, and stayed in England for the rest of his life, apart from a two-year visit to New Zealand in the 1930s. He managed a bookshop in London, and became a fulltime writer in 1951. He wrote eight novels, five of which are set in New Zealand, and many short stories. His writing often centres on family relationships, and the effect that these relationships have on children. His most successful novel, *The Young Have Secrets*, was about a young boy growing up in the time of the First World War.

WITI IHIMAERA

Witi Ihimaera (1944–) was born in Gisborne, New Zealand, and began by writing on the walls of his room in the family home. His first book, a collection of short stories called *Pounamu, Pounamu*, appeared in 1972, and since then he has become one of the best known of all Māori writers. He has published novels and short stories, and won many awards. Writing, for him, is a way of describing to the world what it means to be Māori. He has said that his story *Gathering of the Whakapapa* 'is based on my own grandfather and the time he wanted me to drive him to Murupara to do some work on our tribal genealogy'.

Witi Ihimaera is best known outside New Zealand for *The Whale Rider*, a much loved book published in 1987. This story was made into the film *Whale Rider* in 2003, which won prizes and became a big success all around the world.

PHILIP MINCHER

Philip Mincher (1930—) was born and educated in Auckland. He has written more than fifty short stories, which have been published in journals and anthologies, and he has also published a collection of poems, *Heroes and Clerks*. His stories often reflect his own love of wildlife and the outdoor life. *A Kind of Longing* is part of the story sequence called *The Ride Home*, in which Roy and Kay's love for each other grows against a background of outdoor adventures. Mincher wrote of the sequence: 'I have tried to fix a brief and wonderful time that we all carry within us; to fix a scene with which young people – and older people in memory – can identify.'

JOY COWLEY

Joy Cowley (1936–) found reading difficult as a child, but when she discovered the adventures that could be found in books, she became a reading addict. She began writing stories in the evenings while working as a farmer's wife and bringing up four children. Now she sees herself as a wife, mother, grandmother, and great-grandmother. This is who she is; writing is what she does, and she has been writing for nearly fifty years.

She has written many short stories and novels for adults, more than 600 books for children, and has won a great number of awards. One of her children's books, *Mrs Wishy-Washy's Farm*, has sold more than forty million copies worldwide. She still writes for both children and adults, and spends a lot of time at conferences, workshops, and helping other writers. However, she spends most of her writing time 'answering letters from young friends all over the world, a task that I consider to be more play than work.'

OXFORD BOOKWORMS LIBRARY

Classics • Crime & Mystery • Factfiles • Fantasy & Horror
Human Interest • Playscripts • Thriller & Adventure
True Stories • World Stories

The OXFORD BOOKWORMS LIBRARY provides enjoyable reading in English, with a wide range of classic and modern fiction, non-fiction, and plays. It includes original and adapted texts in seven carefully graded language stages, which take learners from beginner to advanced level. An overview is given on the next pages.

All Stage 1 titles are available as audio recordings, as well as over eighty other titles from Starter to Stage 6. All Starters and many titles at Stages 1 to 4 are specially recommended for younger learners. Every Bookworm is illustrated, and Starters and Factfiles have full-colour illustrations.

The OXFORD BOOKWORMS LIBRARY also offers extensive support. Each book contains an introduction to the story, notes about the author, a glossary, and activities. Additional resources include tests and worksheets, and answers for these and for the activities in the books. There is advice on running a class library, using audio recordings, and the many ways of using Oxford Bookworms in reading programmes. Resource materials are available on the website www.oup.com/elt/bookworms

The *Oxford Bookworms Collection* is a series for advanced learners. It consists of volumes of short stories by well-known authors, both classic and modern. Texts are not abridged or adapted in any way, but carefully selected to be accessible to the advanced student.

You can find details and a full list of titles in the *Oxford Bookworms Library Catalogue* and *Oxford English Language Teaching Catalogues*, and on the website www.oup.com/elt/bookworms

THE OXFORD BOOKWORMS LIBRARY
GRADING AND SAMPLE EXTRACTS

STARTER • 250 HEADWORDS

present simple – present continuous – imperative –
can/cannot, must – *going to* (future) – simple gerunds …

Her phone is ringing – but where is it?

Sally gets out of bed and looks in her bag. No phone. She looks under the bed. No phone. Then she looks behind the door. There is her phone. Sally picks up her phone and answers it. *Sally's Phone*

STAGE 1 • 400 HEADWORDS

… past simple – coordination with *and*, *but*, *or* –
subordination with *before*, *after*, *when*, *because*, *so* …

I knew him in Persia. He was a famous builder and I worked with him there. For a time I was his friend, but not for long. When he came to Paris, I came after him – I wanted to watch him. He was a very clever, very dangerous man. *The Phantom of the Opera*

STAGE 2 • 700 HEADWORDS

… present perfect – *will* (future) – *(don't) have to, must not, could* –
comparison of adjectives – simple *if* clauses – past continuous –
tag questions – *ask/tell* + infinitive …

While I was writing these words in my diary, I decided what to do. I must try to escape. I shall try to get down the wall outside. The window is high above the ground, but I have to try. I shall take some of the gold with me – if I escape, perhaps it will be helpful later. *Dracula*

STAGE 3 • 1000 HEADWORDS
… should, may – present perfect continuous – *used to* – past perfect
– causative – relative clauses – indirect statements …

Of course, it was most important that no one should see Colin, Mary, or Dickon entering the secret garden. So Colin gave orders to the gardeners that they must all keep away from that part of the garden in future. *The Secret Garden*

STAGE 4 • 1400 HEADWORDS
… past perfect continuous – passive (simple forms) –
would conditional clauses – indirect questions –
relatives with *where/when* – gerunds after prepositions/phrases …

I was glad. Now Hyde could not show his face to the world again. If he did, every honest man in London would be proud to report him to the police. *Dr Jekyll and Mr Hyde*

STAGE 5 • 1800 HEADWORDS
… future continuous – future perfect –
passive (modals, continuous forms) –
would have conditional clauses – modals + perfect infinitive …

If he had spoken Estella's name, I would have hit him. I was so angry with him, and so depressed about my future, that I could not eat the breakfast. Instead I went straight to the old house. *Great Expectations*

STAGE 6 • 2500 HEADWORDS
… passive (infinitives, gerunds) – advanced modal meanings –
clauses of concession, condition

When I stepped up to the piano, I was confident. It was as if I knew that the prodigy side of me really did exist. And when I started to play, I was so caught up in how lovely I looked that I didn't worry how I would sound. *The Joy Luck Club*

MORE WORLD STORIES FROM BOOKWORMS

BOOKWORMS · WORLD STORIES · STAGE 1
The Meaning of Gifts: Stories from Turkey
RETOLD BY JENNIFER BASSETT

BOOKWORMS · WORLD STORIES · STAGE 2
Cries from the Heart: Stories from Around the World
RETOLD BY JENNIFER BASSETT
Stories from Nigeria, New Zealand, Botswana, Jamaica,
Uganda, Malaysia, India, South Africa

BOOKWORMS · WORLD STORIES · STAGE 2
Changing their Skies: Stories from Africa
RETOLD BY JENNIFER BASSETT
Stories from Malawi, South Africa, Tanzania

BOOKWORMS · WORLD STORIES · STAGE 3
Dancing with Strangers: Stories from Africa
RETOLD BY CLARE WEST
Stories from South Africa, Tanzania, Uganda

BOOKWORMS · WORLD STORIES · STAGE 4
Doors to a Wider Place: Stories from Australia
RETOLD BY CHRISTINE LINDOP

BOOKWORMS · WORLD STORIES · STAGE 4
Land of my Childhood: Stories from South Asia
RETOLD BY CLARE WEST
Stories from Sri Lanka, India, Pakistan

BOOKWORMS · WORLD STORIES · STAGE 5
Treading on Dreams: Stories from Ireland
RETOLD BY CLARE WEST